wellspring simple

pocket essays

wellspring simple

---

pocket essays

debgrant

✦ ✦ ✦ ✦

Jazzwater

Houston

Wellspring Simple
by Deb Grant

ISBN: 978-0-9824226-9-4
Jazzwater
jazzwater.com
Houston, Texas

Cover Design: *Simple Gifts* by debgrant

To Lisa Hoelscher

Table of Contents

x

Introduction

As an artist, I bounce around in different media. I am glad there is an art form called "mixed media." It describes me and my short attention span. I dabble with watercolor and then switch to acrylic and then to pen and ink and collage. I have the luxury of time to play for which I am grateful. My writing mirrors my hopscotching artistic behavior. I spent 37 years writing sermons and short devotional material. I hopped to poetry, narrative poetry, free style poetry and then to short essays. I decided to call them pocket essays. A pocket essays are a handful of thought, nothing that will strain our pandemic impaired attention span, succinct, to the point with just a hint of mental wandering that one might experience in any free-flowing conversation.

In the late summer of 2021, I started writing these pocket essays which I called *Well of an August Spring.* I wrote on topics that welled up each day from my observations, memories, or readings like waters from an underground spring. The second section of essays I called *Simple Gifts* which highlights those common aspects of life that evoke a sense of gratitude and grace for the living of these less-than-simple days. It is no small gift that you have read the introduction. I am grateful. I hope these pocket essays are a refreshing wellspring on your journey and a lens of insight into your own simple gifts. I have included ways to converse with this book with your own reflections. I hope it sparks conversations with those you with whom you gather.

debgrant

Conversing with WellSpring Simple

I encourage you to converse with this book and use it to kindle conversations in your own life. Here are some possible ways in which this conversation can happen.

A. Individual reading

   This collection of essays has two sections but no particular order. Read cover to cover but feel free to start anywhere, flip through the pages and land wherever you wish.

B. Individual reading with note-taking.

   Some intentional space is built into the format of the book including pages at the back for your own notes. This is a book that encourages you to write in it!

C. Small group conversations.

   + Book group discussions.

   + Conversation starter before meals, meetings or gatherings.

+ Consider using one of these essays to spark a conversation with a friend, family member or co-worker.

+ I invite you to enter into a conversation with me if you wish. My contact information can be found at the end of this book.

Questions to consider as you converse with Wellspring Simple:

1. What stood out for you in this pocket essay?

2. What thoughts or memories surfaced from your own experience?

3. What simple gift similar or different in your own life did this essay evoke for you?

WELLSPRING

Wellspring: Day 1

Once I was obsessed with having an original thought. I wanted the Creator's experience of speaking something out of nothing. Arrogant, yes, but honest. I wanted to invent something totally new. Words are the material of my creations. I can string them together creatively. I thought perhaps I could push the edge of creativity itself and arrange a pattern of words into a thought that has never existed.

My thoughts, however, are the product of other strings of thoughts harvested from a lifetime of reading and listening. My own thought patterns have been shaped by a bombardment of words and images and experiences. It is not possible for me to have an original thought. At best, I could imagine a unique combination of thoughts, colors and patterns. But not that glorious, ex nihilo moment, AHA! There it is my original thought!

Then it occurred to me, like being nudged to awareness by the clearing of a divine throat, that I am an original thought. I am the Creator's original thought. So are you. *I* can't conjure an original thought, but anything created by me is uniquely flavored. That's good. Good enough to put my obsession to rest. ✦

Wellspring: Day 2

Two house finches stood in a small pile of seeds I had put on the patio deck in the morning. The pile was really for the doves who prefer eating off the floor instead of the hanging feeders.

One finch pecked a seed, peeled the husk, swallowed, and repeated the process. The other finch gave its age away by its behavior. It stood in the seed pile not even looking around just tilting its head up, opening its beak, and waiting for the food to drop into its throat. The older finch regarded the gesture of the young one by flicking every third or fourth shucked seed into the clueless one's gaping mouth. It is young. It is still learning. At some point, it will be on its own. At some point, it must and will fend for itself. Some types of birds flock with their own to fend off predators or find their way while migrating. Some gather only to mate and make more birds.

As humans we experience both sides of the seed pile exchange. We fend for ourselves and we tend to our young. But what if our young ones are old enough to fend for themselves? What if those asking for food are not in our flock? Do we direct them to other sources of food or let them take from our pile? When do we graduate from being 'tended to' to 'fending for ourselves?' Human beings can decide what enough is. We can decide that we always have enough to share. It's our choice. ✦

Wellspring: Day 3

I have heard it said that great love and suffering are gateways to great transformation and growth.

I thought of Brian.

He was 5 months old when I met him. He already knew how to generate joy with a sloppy wet grin and sunshine hair in flares that were impossibly soft. His father was my supervising pastor when I was an intern.

"My son will die this year." He told me on our first meeting. Brian was born with organs that could not sustain his life for long. I would be doing the funeral.

Nine months later, Brian died. During those nine months, I was learning to be a pastor, to be present without causing harm, without offering words of comfort all the time. A challenge for me because, after all, I am a word person. The right words fix everything, right? During those nine months, I silently looked through the gateway of great love and suffering embodied by Brian's parents.

Great love and suffering are both present all around us and in us. We often try to embrace the one without the other. I awkwardly fingered through my box of words at Brian's death believing there was a right one I could utter. But our lives, our growth, our transformation into the gift of our humanity is learning when to be completely present in the company of great love and suffering without saying a word. ✦

Wellspring: Day 4

My to-do list is cluttered with one word: de-clutter. I get to a point where the clutter inhibits my ability to think. I detour my movements around the house. I get stuck when all I think about is the clutter, but I have no interest or energy to deal with it so I make another list and consider making the list as an accomplishment.

I've learned that clutter is a significant problem on a global and historic scale. Take the Church, for example. It didn't take long after Jesus did his Middle East tour for Christianity to start collecting beliefs, behaviors, moralities, theologies, philosophies, institutional structures, sausage-making seminaries, hierarchies, litmus tests, altar guilds and building committees.

I get stuck inside all the above-mentioned Christian clutter. The Church is overdue for a purge of theologies and rules that don't love people if they ever did.

The Church in this season is pretty messed up. Lots of clutter. On top of the ancient clutter the Church has accumulated, the task of the clergy and the expectation of the laity have turned us on each other instead of toward those most vulnerable among us. We are all feeling grief and anger.

We can listen to one another. We can stand inside each other's pain and confusion. We can laugh and breathe in each other's joy. We can just as easily drown in our anger and add to each other's clutter.

I am going to stop worrying about the clutter and start paying attention. Today I'll put listening on the top of my to-do list. Maybe tomorrow too. ✦

Wellspring: Day 5

Broadway is coming back. I'm happy for them and us. Eventually the best of Broadway will make its way to the rest of us. Trickle-down theory of theatre.

In college, I double majored in English and biblical studies. I minored in theatre. Live theatre is ancient and thrilling. A window on a world in which we are invited to be voyeurs. Some theatre is so good it draws us in and transforms us at the speed of art, sometimes against our will. My theatre classes covered crucial aspects of the craft including scripts, casting, acting, stage management, directing, costuming, make-up, set design, lighting.

I was fascinated by the economy of set design. How to build without closing off the fourth wall through which the audience peered. How to build a hill or a street or a ship with just enough material to plant the seed of the real thing idea and trust the resource of the viewers' imagination to fill in the rest.

My professor used a couple of exercises to illustrate the way our brains work beyond our will. We were told to draw a map of the mainland United States freehand including all the state borders without looking at a map. Our drawings were childlike and mostly out of proportion. For many of us our brains assume that there are maps at the ready, and we don't need to memorize proportions or how far north is Maine or how far south is Florida or how to make West Virginia fit anywhere.

The other exercise went like this: the professor sternly told us, ordered us, commanded us not to visualize a polar bear riding a tricycle. Our brains ignored the command and offered us visions of fuzzy white bears peddling in our heads.

Our brains can fill in a suggestion of a wall on the stage and help us to focus less on the setting and more on the action of the play. A good thing for the theatre. Our brains also have the capacity to take a suggestion, an unfinished thought, a random story or even a lie and give it a life it was never meant to have. A bad thing for reality.

Broadway lifts us up, helps us laugh. The best of theatre arts tells us the truth. Sitting in the audience, I have observed the joys and the tragedies of how we treat ourselves and each other. Beyond my emotional barricade, I have been invited through the fourth wall to join the actors on stage and look with honesty at my own humanity. Those are the moments when I have walk out of the theatre changed for the better, changed for good. ✦

Wellspring: Day 6

T.S. Eliot wrote the phrase "the still point of the turning world." I love that phrase and I am learning to live it. I believe we are wired to thirst for those moments of stillness in whatever form they take in our trajectories and spinning. The ancient ones called it "sacred time." I think in less lofty terms. Stillpoint brings the image of the Looney Tunes roadrunner to mind. Speed and cunning were vital to the bird's survival to escape the hungry coyote. But the cartoon version of the bird had the ability to find a stillpoint. In the dizzying, circular, desert-dusty chase, the roadrunner could step aside above the fray to be still, observe, heal, learn, and consider its next move.

Even for those serving in professional church capacities, Sunday is rarely ever a stillpoint. For me, my head was going, "what's next, what's next, prepare, check my mic, what page are we on, what is happening in the pew five rows back on the pulpit side, the acolyte is picking his nose, why did I pick this hymn?" Stillpoints happened most often as a happy accident. The light from the stained glass behind my back would drape over my shoulder and pour onto the white altar linen with a prism of color which reduced me to a child saying, "Pretty!" hopefully not out loud into a live mic. The stillpoint might happen in the phrase of a hymn, the chords of music rising to rafters, or a wink of a fellow child at the communion rail. When we stand in that stillpoint no one has to convince us of the value of it. ✦

Wellspring: Day 7

You take the good with the bad. I have heard that all my life. Ying-yang. Highs and Lows. Sinner and Saint. I get it. I get it and then I don't get it. Is it possible to have a learning disability regarding a basic idea such as good and bad? There is good. There is bad. There is a level of maturity when we acknowledge both without all the spin doctoring or under-the-rug sweeping or total denialism. I have developed remarkable skills at avoiding the embracing of both good and bad. I have not been at peace with both. It makes me itch. Perfection is lifted up and embraced as the pinnacle of something. All good, no bad. We fling ourselves on a crusade of vanquishing the bad in and around us. Embracing only the good. When we fail, which we do, then we have to revise the situation to our advantage. No one's perfect, we say, but keep trying. Failure will be forgiven, but only a few times. We can spend a lifetime at war with ourselves.

I splattered on my office wall the Latin phrase "Simul Justus et Peccator" – at the same time, saint and sinner. I knew it held a deep truth within it, BUT

I still wasn't on board. I thought a giant font in wall-sized letters would help. The message of some Christian theologies focuses on the bad, let Jesus die for it, bludgeon it into submission, eradicate it, strive for perfection. A counselor suggested I change my frequent use of BUT to AND to see if that made any difference. It helped AND it wasn't a magical answer. I was more aware of how little elbow room I gave the good stuff before I muscled in a BUT followed by negative thoughts, fears, and preparations for disappointment.

I know there are thousands of volumes written about this concept. Right now there is more than enough negative stuff to add to our sentences after the BUT. I cannot erase the bad stuff. I cannot surgically remove my own negative thinking. I can build up the part of me that has been bullied into submission by the negative voices including my own. I can nurture the muscle that will never be perfect according to my definition AND still is good. I can live with the mess AND lean in to tidy it so that the mess doesn't overwhelm the clean space all the time. Surprisingly, there is a genuine peace inside my own skin when

I have moments when I live with it all. Pigpen of Peanuts is my icon, my hero, my teacher. A dust cloud of dirt, a messy human child. Unclean and wholly at peace with the judgement and pretty good at being a friend and playing baseball. ✦

Wellspring: Day 8

As a child, I took my father's watch apart because I wanted to see how it was made. I thought for sure I could get it back together again just by reversing my steps. It did not go well for the watch or me.

In my defense, I credit and blame my father with my fascination of how things are made. Dad was a foreman in a machine shop that built machines that cut and packaged products like gum, bread and cigarettes. My father would bring us to the shop when a machine was being tested. I got big chunks of gum and a sense of wonder but no cigarettes.

Later in life I made other factory visits. I've seen wallets made. I have seen beer brewed and canned. I smelled 150 proof white lightning dripping through charcoal silos to make sour mash bourbon in a dry county. I felt the heat of molten metal in a foundry making artist's clay visions into bronze. I toured a kayak plant that was a magical combination of brilliant engineering, chemical compounds and hippie artists.

I like to see how things are made. My own art is the product of my wonderings. I will try to make a piece of wooden furniture or paint a picture for no other reason than to see if I can figure out the right components, the order of things and recreate it in my own image, so to speak. It works sometimes. Never perfectly. My sense of wonder swirls in different mediums. I love the paper and the paints, the brushes and the pens, the wood grains and the carving tools as much as I enjoy the finished piece.

It occurs to me that we are still being made. As humans we are uniquely invited to participate in the process. We can tinker with it. More quickly I am recognizing that it won't always go well nor will it be flawless. Leaning into the process means we will learn something, even in our failures, and put our names with a sense of humility and pride to the humans we are becoming. ✦

Wellspring: Day 9

A Roman Catholic missionary told a story about teaching a tribe of people far removed from western civilization. The priest explained to his students that there are seven sacraments – an event where God is was present. The students were shocked and confused. They wanted to know, "Why so few?" Their own experience of divine presence and mystery, something greater than themselves, happened much more frequently.

When the Protestant Reformation came along to push back against hierarchical powers and corruption, the number of sacraments was reduced from seven to two. Baptism and Holy Communion apparently were the only two places where the divine presence touches earthly elements and humans. I like the idea that the church is willing to critique itself and make necessary changes. I question our overreach in defining and counting what is holy.

On a bright day, I stood outside the Wieskirche – a pilgrimage church in a valley of the Bavarian Alps in Germany. Inside the centuries old sanctuary was a visual explosion of rococo art, cherub baby bottoms, gold leaf covered carvings. The ceilings and walls were covered in pastel paintings depicting the stories of Genesis as soft soap operas and heavenly cerulean skies, benevolent clouds, mostly sunny with only a ten percent chance of rain. The pilgrimage church was built with offerings collected by church officials who promised that traveling to one of these sacred structures would bring them closer to God. After I toured the sacred interior, I walked outside. I took in the overwhelming, soaring beauty of the snow-cover mountain peaks against a real blue sky with the impossible green meadows at their foothills. The church was beautiful and touched by God and humans. But there is so much more and God is not finished.

Look! There's another sacrament! And another... ✦

Wellspring: Day 10

I've heard the analogy that growing in relationship with God is like falling in love. I have had little as a frame of reference in that regard, but my experience has provided me a unique vantage point.

I worked in campus ministry for a large part of my career. Unlike strictly parish ministry, the people with whom I worked were literally and figuratively constantly changing. Campus ministry is like looking through a window to a view of a river. I could only see a small part of the river. I didn't know much about where it had been or where it was going. I was present to it for the short time it was in the sight of my window. I encountered these mysterious humans as they lived the short and formative years of their college journey. They experienced freedom of adult choices and the possibilities of different career paths and partners. I learned that in campus ministry I had to love the students quickly. They would be out of range of my river window soon enough. Grace is served in loving them quickly. Those I didn't love quickly enough, I didn't serve them well. I also knew the heartbreak of saying goodbye. The time of being in life with them if only for that short rush of river rapids was a privilege. They richly shaped my understanding of joy and love and God. They were, and many still are, my bread and wine.

One of the college towns I lived and worked in for several years lacked any terrain worthy of note. No grand architecture though some would argue for the football stadium. No large body of water. No elevation. No stand of tall trees. Its character came from the people and the reputation of the university. One day a student was telling me about the person he was dating. He said, "I know I am in love." I had witnessed this one person date many people but the certainty in his voice startled me. Having little personal experience, I blurted out the typical question: "How do you know?" He said, "Because even this town looks beautiful to me."

Love has a power that should not be underestimated. There is some wisdom in choosing to love one another quickly so that the whole world, everything and everyone, looks beautiful. Even now. Even now. ✦

Wellspring: Day 11

Ed Yong is the science writer for *The Atlantic*. His articles are good. Well-researched. Thoughtful. Most of all, they inform me. They change me. They give me hope even with the blunt facts. His agenda is to tell the truth, and he genuinely cares about humans. After he won the Pulitzer for his pandemic articles, I wrote to congratulate him and thank him. I know how fan mail works. It goes nowhere. It just makes the sender feel good to try to make a connection. I wrote it anyway because it seemed good. Shortly after, I received a message from Ed Yong. I don't know if it was through a staff person or Ed Yong directly. The message referenced phrases from my note to him in his response. I chose to believe it was truly Ed Yong and not some sophisticated algorithm to mimic a personal touch of communication.

This is what I believe. A note was sent without deep expectation to let a writer know his work sparked a change in a single human. The writer wrote back. A tiny human circuit was completed. Like a completed electrical circuit, the energy had a conduit, and the energy was charged with human goodness. I feasted on that spark of goodness. I still do just telling you about it. It feels like putting bare feet in the ground and letting the earth love you back.

I am not ready to cut the cable on humans, though the temptation is great. There is a virus out there that has usurped our human conduits to keep its poisonous self alive. It is making us sick and killing us. There is life out there, though. We can build new conduits to tap into the life. It seems good to listen for signals of human ingenuity and kindness and complete that circuit with whatever we have on hand. Gratitude is always handy. ✦

Wellspring: Day 12

Scarcity happens and triggers fear. Scare is embedded in scarcity. It is defined in fundamental economic principles of supply and demand. When demand overwhelms supply, it creates the condition of not enough. Not enough water. Not enough hospital beds. Not enough staff. Not enough money. Not enough time. Not enough patience. Not enough energy.

Scarcity triggers fear triggers survival instincts. Me, mine, mine, mine. From toilet paper to land to individual freedom to time to power. When will it be our turn? When will we be first in line? When will we be someone's first priority? There is only so much time and attention to go around. Only so much love. So we circle around and hoard what is ours. It's natural. It's economics.

If we value compassion toward the stranger and the value of our instinct to protect ourselves and our family, then we have to face our fear of scarcity. It is possible. I think it is possible. I want to believe it is possible. It may require invasive surgery to graft the spirit of compassion to the vein that feeds our neurons and our flesh. And then there is the problem of compassion fatigue. I have witnessed it. I have felt the shame of it. Caring can be exhausting. There doesn't seem to be enough...enough love to go around.

What if we faced our fear of not having enough, one fear at a time. Compassion is not a commodity on a stock exchange. It won't run out if we are facing our fears together. The feeding of the 5000 on the hills of Galilee was not magical supply to meet the demand. It was an act of compassion by people who discovered what they could do if they weren't afraid of not having enough. ✦

Wellspring: Day 13

The Big Lie. I hate that phrase. It is defined these days as the political pouting of a boy-man and his minions.

It is not The Big Lie. Not even close.

Jimmy had a slight build, a tender face, a southern voice of a Carolina gentleman with plush black hair that evoked the instinct to pet his head because it looked so soft. He played the trumpet though he was a quiet man. He took on one of the most difficult degree programs at the university. He was the first in his family to attend college. He followed the students in a campus ministry group to pizza, pubs and mountain trails. We loved him as best we could. It was hard. He walked in darkness. He was drowning in it. The ancient method of stoning as execution was not always throwing stones at the accused. It involved the person laying on the ground, under a wide board and having boulders the size of basketballs placed slowly on the board until the person was crushed to death. That is what some describe as depression. A slow death. The boulders are invisible and so we think they lack volume. Jimmy was the accused and the accuser. He was being crushed by the weight of real pain. The weight was measured not in pounds but lies. The disease of depression built a wall of darkness on him and around him until he was defenseless against the lies. The lie that said he was inadequate as a son to his family, as a friend, as a human taking up space on the planet, that life contained too much pain for any reason to continue being in it.

He withdrew from school. He hugged me goodbye. He whispered in my ear, "You did the best you could." At his father's house, in the darkness, Jimmy walked to the middle of the yard so that he wouldn't make a mess in the house and shot himself.

Jimmy believed the Big Lie and he wanted to deal with it alone. And he did.

The Big Lie is dangerous and threatening. It has little to do with puny men with too much power.

I heard the definition of an honorable life as keeping what is true in view. To honor becomes an ethic we learn to live by. TO LIVE by. When I honor myself, I keep what I know to be true about myself in view especially when I am troubled or feeling lost and believing the lie.

To honor others who are diminished in their capacity to maneuver in the darkness is to reach out to them, care for them, to feed them slivers of the moonlight. Life becomes measured not in years or accomplishments but in small kindnesses, a human minute at a time. A little bit of moonlight will not keep those who walk in darkness alive forever, but it may keep them alive until morning. ✦

Wellspring: Day 14

I lived in Maine for a couple years after college, before seminary. A friend invited me out to her place at the lake, and she gave me a quick course on how to sail her small sailboat. It was not complicated. I had been out sailing with her several times already and knew how things worked. I looked forward to taking it out by myself while she went into town to run some errands. The air felt clean, sharp, and crisp like crunching into a perfectly ripe apple. I tacked neatly across the lake and enjoyed the wind slicing the little boat through the chilly waters that were the first thing to take on the touch of fall, which always came too quickly in Maine. The side of the boat rose out of the water, and I leaned my body straight over the edge and felt like I was inside the perfect poster for the joys of sailing. I liked the little boat. I liked my little life. But the wind picked up suddenly and the boat tipped further and the speed increased beyond my comfort level. I heard my friend's calm instruction in my head: "If you ever feel you are losing control of the boat, just let go of the mainsheet, the rope holding the main sail, and the boat will turn into the wind and stop."

"Just let go of the mainsheet," I repeated to myself as I felt my hand grip the rope even tighter. In that millisecond of time I knew that my friend was far more experienced at sailing than I was and her word could be trusted. I knew that she would not want fear to disturb the enjoyment of my sailing experience. I knew that she would not want me to die. I also knew that holding on meant that I was in control.

Letting go meant that the boat and the wind and forces I didn't understand would be in control. Letting go made absolutely no sense to me when holding on meant I was in control. I ignored the best advice, and I trusted my own instinct. I did not let go. I held on.

Within seconds I was dumped into the cold lake. I thrashed around finally flinging half my body on the underside of the sailboat that was now completely upside down with an open sail underwater—practically an impossible situation to correct by myself. A small boy in a motorboat started making lazy circles around me as I dangled wet and cold from my little shipwreck. He finally shouted to me asking if I needed any help. Even I knew that this was not a moment when my fierce sense of independence was going to do me any good. I let go. I sucked up my pride and let this child, who was laughing throughout the experience, tow me and my tangled little boat back to the dock.

Letting go is one of the most difficult lessons of my life. I HATE that I had to type that sentence in the present tense. Life is full of letting go. It doesn't get easier. The best we can do is get a little quicker at seeing what we have to do and at trusting the voices of those who love us. Quicker at gutting it up and letting go. ✦

Wellspring: Day 15

Humility is complicated. That's my excuse for when I don't want to admit a weakness. Humility's throne is never in danger. It is often literally a throne. The toilet seat. It is the place where the name of God is spoken the most often with humility and sincerity.

I was invited to join a seminary friend on a visit to a cousin's sheep farm. I knew nothing about sheep. It was a rainy, winter day and the herd was mostly gathered underneath a large open wooden pavilion. The farmer was a tall man, and as he moved among the sheep, he had to bow his head so as not to hit it on the rafters. Trying to be funny, I asked him why, given his height, he built the roof on the shelter so low. He said, "It is not that I built the roof so low, it is that I haven't had the time recently to muck it out. The roof isn't low. It's the sheep that built the floor so high." I think I caught him smiling to himself the moment he saw the look on my face when it dawned on me what I was standing on.

Humility. Toilets. Oh, God. Maybe that is what we are all standing in right now. Maybe our best hope is mucking out our own shit. ✦

Wellspring: Day 16

There are some stories that were passed down to us through the ages and have a way of welling up at times when we most need to hear them again.

Such a story goes like this:

When faced with a particularly weighty problem, the Baal Shem Tov, founder of Hasidic Judaism, would go to a certain place in the woods, light a sacred fire, and pray. In this way, he found insight into his dilemma. His successor, Rabbi Dov Ber, followed his example and went to the same place in the woods and said, "The fire we can no longer light, but we can still say the prayer." And he, too, found what he needed. Another generation passed, and Rabbi Moshe Leib of Sassov went to the woods and said, "The fire we can no longer light, the prayer we no longer remember; all we know is the place in the woods, and that will have to suffice." And it did. In the fourth generation, Rabbi Israel of Rishin stayed at home and said, "The fire we can no longer light, the prayer we no longer know, nor do we remember the place. All we can do is tell the tale." And that, too, proved sufficient. ✦

Even when we don't know where to go, what to do, what to pray, how to help, there is something truly healing about telling stories and listening to one another. ✦

Wellspring: Day 17

Early in my grade school history lessons about noteworthy people, I began to see a common thread that was curious and disturbing. Many of these people had experienced suffering. The suffering and their response to it set them on a trajectory for the rest of their lives. It has been a lesson in progress to this day.

One day, I had a conversation with college students about who in their lives represented a strong faith – not just Bible verse memorizers or pulpit thumpers, but those who embodied a profound grace and belief in this gift of life. Many of the students said their grandparents. When I asked them what would it take to have faith like their grandparents, they were silent until one young woman spoke quietly and then loud enough for all to hear. "We would have to suffer, " she said." We would have to suffer and learn to live a life of grace with the pain." She said the words as if she was seeing for the first time how little she herself had suffered in her life and that, in her human journey ahead, there lurked untold suffering. The wisdom of her words hung in the air like the stillness of an empty cathedral.

That moments of suffering happen to one and all is not unusual in the human story. What matters is how we respond. ✦

Wellspring: Day 18

Before seminary, I worked in a city hospital as an assistant librarian and the only person in the hospital who knew how to operate a film projector. It was my job to run the birth film for the prenatal classes. I got tired of watching this baby in the film being born again and again. After showing a film of a C-section procedure and the audience had left, I ran the film backwards. In reverse, the film started with the doctor examining the baby, re-attaching the umbilical cord, stuffing the baby back into the womb through the incision, and zipping the mother back up.

I think about that film clip whenever it occurs to me that as a species human beings are not "fully cooked" as it were. When something we are baking in our kitchens looks undone, we can bake it a few more minutes. This metaphor is pretty cruel on the human level to pregnant women who don't need to be equated with an oven and are more than ready to get that baby out to face the world. So forgive me. My choice in metaphors sometimes proves my point. I, too, am not fully cooked.

Sometimes I just wish we humans were not the most destructive creatures on the planet. Sometimes I wish we could have a do-over. Sometimes I wish that being born again wasn't a hijacked phrase that has had the truth trampled out of it. I wish growing up was as easy as hitting the rewind button. It's not. Backwards is not a good option. The way forward doesn't need to be all bad. ✦

Wellspring: Day 19

When talking about setting dates for events and making plans in the midst of the pandemic, a friend said, "We schedule events with the understanding we hold things loosely."

These are the times when the only thing that seems absolutely certain is uncertainty. We hold things loosely. Be prepared to let go.

In recent days, I have:

+Witnessed friends let go of their children to the adventure and the uncertainty of public schools and college campuses.

+Witnessed a friend let go of a constant furry companion of 19 years.

+Witnessed a friend live inside the uncertain health and the inevitability of an aging parent.

+A favorite coffee shop too crowded for me to frequent with comfort.

+An air conditioner that needed to be repaired in the Texas heat with funds that insist on being held loosely.

+Witnessed the news – an encyclopedia of uncertainty.

+My attention called to another storm in the gulf. I hold the projection of the storm's path loosely. And prepare in case it wobbles and slams nearby.

We hold things loosely.

There are days when I would just settle for being held. ✦

Wellspring: Day 20

"Tell me the story of the day I was born." It is the story I wanted to hear frequently as a child. Not that it was a great tale, but I was hoping it would get better in the re-telling. It was a story inflicted upon me unsolicited as a teenager.

What I was told about the day I was born from my father was very little. He did what was expected of men at the time. He drove his wife to the hospital. He sat in a waiting room. Sometime later, he picked his wife and his daughter up at the hospital and drove us home. I learned the day after he died, I was not his first daughter. I met her at Dad's funeral.

What I was told about the day I was born from my mother was painful. Apparently, I wanted to be born on August 1st but the doctor was drunk. I finally decided I couldn't wait any longer and was born on August 2nd at 2:00 am into the arms of a less than sober physician. Mother was thrilled I was a girl. She already had two boys. I would be her first girl but not her last. I spent my first days in a chest of drawers because of the lack of funds for a baby bed. When I was a teenager, Mother added the details of a great deal of hemorrhaging that I had caused her.

I don't remember. I don't remember being hungry, having wet diapers, sleeping in a drawer, meeting the family, being held or discovering my feet.

There is a certain grace I appreciate about not having memories of the first years of my life. It was messy and seriously uncomfortable, and it gave me plausible deniability when it came to any felony I may have committed on landing. ✦

Wellspring: Day 21

Do you remember the moment of recognition of a life lesson, a moment of truth?

I've had several. Sometimes the truth was the same as a previous one, but I needed a refresher course. One of those moments happened to me on August 28, 2017, 8:57 pm.

I know the time thanks to the wonder of a text message that I received and kept.

Hurricane Harvey had parked itself over the Texas and dumped over 50 inches of rain in short order overwhelming waterways, flooding homes, cars and businesses. The church I was serving at the time of Harvey was inundated with four feet of flood water. Standing inches away from the television, I touched the screen when the national news showed the main street near the church. Until the water receded, I couldn't get near it. I needed a plan to help the congregation move forward even as most of them were dealing with their own flooded homes. I felt powerless, vulnerable and over my head.

I loathe asking for help. There is a river of independence running rapidly in my veins since my childhood. It served me well at times. It was dangerous and foolish at other times.

I got a text message from an Episcopal colleague down the road. Their church had escaped the immediate flood. Many months later they would discover their own flood damage in the floors and walls but until then, they opened their dry island to the townspeople. My colleague offered worship space for as long as needed to our church family who would not be able to gather in its buildings again for over a year.

Trusting my colleague's compassion helped even though she was as overwhelmed as I was by the damage and the suffering before us. As hard as it was to say "yes" to an offer of help, I had to shove aside my individualist upbringing. I needed help. My congregation needed help. It was a no brainer to say yes. At least, until the next disaster. I hope I remember we are in it together. ✦

Wellspring: Day 22

I read an article about broken wells on failing farms. The owners of farms that need the water for their crops during a drought often believe that the well is the problem. It just needs to have a part replaced and then it will be running again. Often, that is the quick but costly fix the engineer can offer with the warning: it won't last long. There is a bigger problem. There isn't enough water to go around. To meet demand, more acres are planted that need more water. It is unsustainable with a change that goes beyond a replacement part for well pump.

The Butterfly effect is a theory loosely defined as the air current off the wings of a butterfly that incrementally grows over one land mass into a disturbance of clouds over an ocean into a hurricane on another coast. One small action triggers and accumulates into an impactful event effecting millions of lives. A virus. An armed conflict. All have small beginnings and with the right environment reach devastating proportions.

I just finished eating a biscuit made of almond flour. Almond trees require an enormous amount of water to produce a small crop. I am a part of the demand chain for more almonds. I am a butterfly flapping its wings. I don't know what a single butterfly can do to stop a hurricane, a single health care worker can do to halt a virus, a single soldier can do to end a war. I do know some basic economics. We will do what we have the resources to do and then when those resources dry up we will make the changes necessary to save our own lives. It doesn't have to be this way. It takes widening our field of vision. We don't do that when we are scared. It takes compassion from an unlimited source. Such a source exists, and we haven't even begun to know the depths of that well. ✦

Wellspring Day: 23

I heard a person suggest to me to find yourself a true place.

A true place for me is standing barefoot on the edge of an ocean. It is that moment for me when I am utterly overwhelmed and completely at peace with the paradox of my insignificance and my greatness.

At such a time as this, we stand with our spiritual toes in an ocean of joy and grief, order and chaos, compassion, and cruelty within us and around us. What comes next? I don't know.

Until then, find yourself a true place. I trust we all have something like a tuning fork in our souls that helps us identify our true place. If you don't know what your true place is, I trust in time you will.

Find yourself a true place. Linger there a bit. It is what I wish the most for you. ✦

SIMPLE

Simple Gifts: Morning Routine

Daybreak is a gift. The sun rising is a giant reset button that never bores me. I lean into the little routine sparked by the closest star and a spinning planet. I have known many for whom the rising sun is not hopeful. I understand. Depression can be more formidable than the dark monsters underneath our beds. For me, daybreak is a gift and the gift comes in the morning routine.

The gift is the new day and the routine.

Mine starts with the awareness of awakeness. This means I have slept which is cause for celebration even in little bits. The morning starts with the muscle memory of gratitude. I am grateful to be alive. I didn't die before I awoke as the child's bedtime prayer suggests. My soul is still mine.

This gift strips off its own wrappers. My little dog is in my face threatening to pee on my sheets. My own bladder is threatening to pee on my sheets. My dog waits with whining for my toilette noises to end. Then comes the donning of my shorts and shirt and shoes.

I approach the stairs with care. I have no interest in upsetting my routine with 9-1-1. My pet parrot says, "Good Morning!" That's what I want you to believe. My bird greets me most often with the F-bomb. Lord knows where he heard it. I start the water for the coffee. I take the dog outside to fertilize the grass. I let the weather slap me with coolness or hungry mosquitoes or the hot hands of Texas coast humidity.

I feed my bird. I feed my dog and then prepare my food. Someone said that breakfast was the least changed meal of the day. I like not having to think too much in the morning and don't want to cook too much. I thank God for the inventor of the microwave. I then get on a "thank you" roll for pre-cooked sausage and almond flour biscuits. I am thankful for coffee beans which render their magic.

Before I unfast with my daybreak food, I fill a plastic cup with sunflower seeds and peanuts for squirrels, jays, doves and cardinals. The little birds have their own feeders. They all arrive about the time I sit at the window. Knowing what's coming, my parrot makes the noise of my first tender slurp before I even taste my coffee.

Simple gift of a morning routine. I'll bet you have one, too. Perhaps more difficult and jarring, but routine, nevertheless. The dark monsters of the night are not vanquished, but there really is a joy in the morning of a new day even if the joy only lasts as long as it takes for our to-do lists to knock rudely. There is joy sometimes even if it is only a dog who needs to pee and a bird with a potty mouth. I read this morning that "God is great and everywhere today." Yes, indeed. ✦

Simple Gifts: Photosynthesis

I grow sprouts. Broccoli sprouts to be precise. My various attempts at growing actual food on my deck has resulted in a small but charming herb patch. The mint, I learned from a lady who knows her herbs like every kid in the neighborhood, is the playground bully. Best to give it plenty of space and keep it away from the other children. I also had a pepper plant which critters ate to the roots. My tomato plant has been lovely. I thoroughly enjoyed the harvest of one tomato. I asked a friend who knows far more than I do regarding plants if my tomato plant needed to get laid. He said, "No, it gets pollinated by the wind. It does NOT like Texas summer heat so give it time." He was right. It cooled off. For Texas standards that means high 80s. I now have three tomatoes. But all that led me to become a sprout farmer.

Broccoli sprouts have a nutty flavor and crunch and lots of good nutrients. They can be grown indoors in small batches. My kind of farming, though even with refrigeration keeping anything fresh in my house is a challenge. I did my research. I checked out the most popular DIY models of sprouts in a canning jar to expensive contraptions with lights and water sensors with seed pads which looked like green diapers. I went with an excellent stainless-steel model that looks like two round cake pans. One pan has a steel mesh filter on the bottom to facilitate spraying the sprouting seeds twice a day. More importantly, it is easy to keep clean. A major factor for me even if it does make me sound like a housewife in a 1950's commercial.

Ah yes, back to simple gifts and broccoli sprouts. With only small attention on my part, every week or so I get to witness little dead round seeds suck up water, shuck their caskets and grow white fibers of wet tenderness up and down. I did not have to teach them up and down. Each seed comes with its own database of how to make leaves without any direction from me. When they are about two inches tall, I make them stand in the doorway and put pencil marks on the wall. After they roll their leaves at me, they get to continue growing in the sunlight. I mess with them a little by turning the tray away from the window where they point their little leafy heads as if they were all at Springsteen concert. Within a few hours they are pointed to the sun again and greener by the minute. Photosynthesis! Chlorophyll! I paid just enough attention in science class to be amazed, to trust it and to be humbled by all the cool stuff happening under the sun and my nose.

Then I get to eat them. This is good. Sprouts are food not friends. If I kept them too long I would give them names and dress them in Halloween costumes as mint bullies. And yes, there is a sense of pride in eating something I have grown myself even though I had VERY little to do with the hard parts. I just gave it space and water and light. And even those three things are a gift. ✦

Simple Gifts: Fin

When the salt water of the coastal bay is carried by tides and changing currents into estuaries, dolphins venture further up into rivers feeding the bay. That explains the logic of the sighting, but not the exaltation of it.

Small fish leap occasionally. The sea birds hover and plunge then float while they swallow. A broken piece of pier drifts. Each with their own shape breaks the surface of the water. The water itself is shaped by the wind or the lack of it. But then...

"Did you see that?"

"No, what?"

And then it happens for my eyes, too. A dolphin fin. Sometimes the fin appears with the silhouette of a nose and a tail gliding and gone. The purest reaction is glee. To share the planetary space of water and air with such grace is a gift. Long after the fins are out of sight, you keep looking. The fact of seeing them feeds hope. Hope is hungry to believe goodness happens and will happen again. It is good to keep looking. Delight happened before. It can happen again. Let's keep looking. ✦

Simple Gifts: Open Door

A stranger held a door open for me at the post office. Later in the day, I held a door open for a stranger at the coffee shop. There was a civility about the gesture received and given. A simple act of opening and holding a door would not normally glisten. I wondered why? Why was it remarkable? Why did it feel good for me to open the door later at the coffee shop?

After months of being separated from people behind closed doors, this gesture felt personal and familiar. After a long season of fear and frustration of keeping our distance, this opening of a door felt like the way home to being in public again, to being neighbors. We have not lost the sublime tenderness of being human.

Opening a door for a stranger or walking through a door held open for us will not solve the problems we still face together. It may just be a familiar gesture that reminds of our ability to be just and kind to all who face a closed door. ✦

Simple Gifts: Stars

There is so much I can't do with stars. I can't count them, at least, not accurately. I can't own them. I can't name them all. I can't touch them. I can't take them out of a vault to stir my neighbor's envy. I can't always see them. Yet on a night polluted with streets lights or hidden by clouds, they are always there. "Steadfast as Keats' Eremite," wrote Robert Frost when pleading with us to choose something like a star to steady us in times of chaos.

Through the ages, the stars have sparked stories, guided travelers, companioned our journeys and received our wishes. We arrange them into constellations to find them in the sky, and they do come again. Orion's Belt passes over the bow of my deck as surely as the flight path of airplanes or migrating pelicans.

When I take my little dog outside before bedtime, I look up and see stars. I feel not isolated but in rich company. I feel not scarcity but abundance.. I look up to know wealth that I will never own but will always have. ✦

Simple Gifts: Scars

It is a great icebreaker. Tell the story of one of your scars. We all have them. They all have stories. THAT we have them is itself a gift – the body's ability to mount a defense against a wound. Sometimes stitches help it along, but our biology does the heavy lifting. Then the stories scars evoke speak of accidents, mistakes, surgeries, assaults. Many fit into the category of "it seemed like a good idea at the time."

I have a scar on my leg from the exhaust pipe of a motorcycle. One on my palm from piercing chestnuts to string for the Christmas tree. Another replaces the pattern of my fingerprint with a spot left when I cut off the tip with a woodcarving knife. Our belly buttons are scars of necessary separation. Some scars look healed, but the stories are less so.

Scars remind us of our physical resilience and mark our flesh with scrapbook memories that are ours to tell or not. ✦

Simple Gifts: Hands

Hawkeye Pierce in the M*A*S*H series did a lovely, short soliloquy about the miracle of the human hand with its opposable thumbs. A hand is a remarkable feat of biological engineering literally at our fingertips. Our hands are versatile. They are capable of many different actions.

There are hands attached to hearts I know in Minnesota. Over the years, they have traveled to disaster sites to help rebuild homes. Their fingerprints are on hundreds of walls, floors, water pipes and electrical circuits. When the pandemic limited the ability to gather, those same hands built children's desks for families in need. When it still wasn't possible to travel to disaster damaged homes, those hands connected to those big hearts were itchy for action. They formed a Chore Corps like a tiny National Guard... to prepare and respond to local neighbors who needed an extra hand with chores like pulling weeds, washing windows, repairing stairs.

Hands can form a church and build a steeple, but only when they open the doors from the inside out will they ever see all the people who need a hand. Hands, by themselves, are a wonder of creation. Connected to a source of love, hands make healing happen. ✦

Simple Gifts: Barefoot

When was the last time you took off your shoes and stood barefoot on the earth? I had to think about it. Inside the house, padding around doesn't count. Sandals or stocking feet or flip flops don't count. Concrete sidewalk or the patio or pool deck doesn't count either. When was the last time you stood barefoot on soil, sand, grass, or rocks?

I have the luxury of living within a short drive from a beach and within walking distance of grassy areas near a lake. I have rich barefoot opportunities. I am, according to a friend, a barefoot wimp. I like to keep my feet in the lap of shoe luxury. I whine about pieces of seashells. On grass, fire ants are an honest fear where I live. If you've never met one, think of tiny picnic ants with a hornet disposition, home-grown terrorists that can marshal the troops in seconds. I have allowed pedi-comfort and the fear of fire ants to distance me from any intimate connection to the earth. I have to admit that the connection is pulsing with mystery. Some explain the connection in terms of particles and electrons. Some explain it in terms of earth as our mother. Some dismiss it as a placebo effect or tree-huggerism.

Nevertheless, I am willing to stand bravely barefooted a bit more often these days. I am still a tender foot, but I do tell my feet to toughen up like telling a child to take their medicine or eat their vegetables. I honestly don't know how to explain it nor will I dismiss it. I just know that standing barefoot on the earth is a simple gift that does something good. ✦

Simple Gifts: Color

I play with colors. I am only now learning how they get along and what happens when they don't. Having the right tools for distribution of the colors helps: crayons, pens, pencils, markers, and brushes. What the pigment is liquified in matters: water, oil, alcohol. And then there is blending hues and choosing palettes. The vast chasm of my lack of knowledge extends before me like the Grand Canyon torturing me with variations of colors I am clueless to know how to reproduce or blend.

There are people whose job it is to name colors for paint. There is another company that chooses the "Color of the Year" and suggests a palette that clothes and interior designers scramble to highlight in their creations.

Some colors work well together, complement contrasting warmth and coolness, or convey a mood or a landscape. Other colors when mixed become mud as if they gave up the fight, lost their identity and died, returning to the earth from which they all came.

Flesh tones could be a crayon box of many hues instead of a single beige one named "Flesh." We see what we want to see. We are often asked our favorite color.

Color blindness as a metaphor is a defensive comment dropped into conversations, a person claiming to be color-blind might do so as a way to show how fair they are in the treatment of all people. I am not so sure the argument works. Instead of equalizing differences, it dampens the vibrant identity that makes us unique. Actual color-blindness is a quirk of genetics, not a life-choice we can claim as a free pass from doing the hard work of real justice.

I have watched dozens of videos of people with the physical disability of color blindness as they are gifted with glasses that help them distinguish colors. Their response is always the same. They cry. They weep for the intoxicating world of color. They weep for all the truth they were missing and can now embrace. If only there were such glasses that could help us see through the fog of our misconceptions and prejudices to behold the truth we have missed in our human stories and can now embrace.

Colors are a gift. How we cherish and behold them matters. ✦

Simple Gifts: Indoor Plumbing

Oh, I know. There is nothing simple about indoor plumbing. There is a vast infrastructure of ditches, pipes, pumps, waste management, skilled labor, utility finances, water districts, regulatory bodies, fixture manufacturers, and engineers involved in making my morning toilette a simple journey.

One thing I can cross off my bucket list is having done my business in an outhouse on ranch land while on a camping retreat. You haven't lived until you have felt the prairie winds of Texas riding up your bare butt while you are trying to be quick about the necessary activity without impaling your lower cheeks with splinters. In this situation, men have a personal plumbing advantage. For me, however, it was this experience that made indoor plumbing glisten for years to come.

The fact is indoor plumbing is a complicated wonder of multi-disciplines of infrastructure. The simple part is never, ever being ungrateful. ✦

Simple Gifts: Acorn Day

A friend of mine has a name for a moment that stops you and shines with goodness...the feeling of being at the right place at the right time. Walking a tree lined path on campus, he tells the story of when an acorn fell from tree, bounced on the sidewalk and into his open palm. The little moment splashed with surprise. It interrupted the trajectory of his thoughts with joy. It released a grateful response. Now he has a name for all the moments before or since that were full of effervescent blessing. He call it "An Acorn Day."

I read today of a woman who was woken in the night by an explosive noise, a hole through the roof and ceiling above her bed, and a 2.8-pound meteorite near her pillow.

Surprise, interruption, joy and gratitude. We all have these moments though we rarely name them. Acorn Day sounds a little less life-threatening than the Day a Rock From Outer Space Crashed Through My Roof Missing Me by Inches. The fact we are still alive to tell the stories of surprise, interruption, joy and gratitude is really good. Even better to give those moments a name in case we forget what a gift they are. What would you name a moment like that for you? ✦

Simple Gifts: Flavor

Food is a necessity. Certainly, it is innately a gift because food originates from the earth which is the mother of gifts. But food doesn't have to have flavor to deliver its necessary function. Flavor is a gift. Sweet, savory, spicy, salty. My dog must like my flavor. She licks my legs. I am grateful she doesn't want to eat them.

My tastes have changed over the years. I used to like Twinkies. I don't anymore. I would rather have key lime pie now. A salt-free diet driven by health concerns is damaging to one's mental health. The incendiary levels of one's chili are litmus tests for bravado. Cooking shows are challenged to find players who can with words and actions make the audience salivate for the dish they can neither taste nor smell. Covid-19 can rob its victims of both smell and taste for short or extended periods of time.

I have been harvesting one tiny cherry tomato about once a week. I used to be frustrated that the harvest was not more plentiful. Now I am grateful that once a week I get to have a moment in which I am intentionally motivated to savor the flavor of a single tiny tomato. If

I am really lucky, I get to share one with a neighbor, not like in a salad, but more like holy communion...but with more flavor than those wafers. ✦

Simple Gifts: Compliment

I give compliments. I receive them. Gift is the nature of a compliment. Criticism isn't so clear. When given for the sake of belittling, it stings. I have been the victim of harsh critique. It saps my energy to marshal a defense against the pain. It was work to sift through the brutal offering to find a constructive bit of golden truth that might have been well-intended but crassly delivered. I have done my share of delivering criticism without caring how it was received only that I had my say. Another reason the pain of criticism lingers is because of its specificity such as a quirk of my personality or a threat to my current or future employment. Compliments rarely pack such a punch. The words used are vague, lighter than the household dust floating briefly visible in the sunlight. I dismiss them. They do not stick with me. They are not anesthetic for me against the criticism.

The ancient poet Hafiz once wrote, "A sincere wanting and need to artfully give is inherent in love. And love gets its way; for patience it knows, and what a strength that is...we have a chance to help paint each other gold."

The gift of a compliment for the giver involves love, patience to collect and observe the specifics. A well-crafted compliment requires enough selflessness to pay attention to the other. An artful delivery helps so that the recipient cannot dismiss it easily but feels the motivation of our love and the heft of our sincerity. We do indeed have "the chance to paint each other gold." ✦

Simple Gifts: Pocket

I wear more pants than dresses. Pants almost always have pockets. Dresses almost never do. I like pockets. Always have. My father felt like corduroy and a five o'clock shadow. Soft and rough. I stole his corduroy shirt from his closet after he died. I wore it thread-bare and saved the chest pocket.

During my working years, my pocket carried a honey-lemon lozenge. A preacher's necessity to wet the tongue and throat. There is an old joke about the preacher who spoke without notes and ended his sermon only when his lozenge was melted completely. One Sunday he reached into his pocket and popped a button into his mouth by mistake. He just kept talking. He died in the pulpit.

I carried a Susan B. Anthony dollar coin in my pocket for a long time because I never believed I would ever see a woman on an American coin. I knew a grandma who carried hard candies in her pockets for the grands. Insurance for their excited greeting. It worked.

Now when I am inside the house, my pockets carry a favorite pen and a bit of paper to catch thoughts I drop from room to room. My pockets carry seeds and biscuits for my bird and dog respectively. When I go out, I check my pockets for mask, wallet, keys, and phone. Sometimes, I skip the phone. The statue of Johann Sebastian Bach in the courtyard outside of St. Thomas Church in Leipzig depicts Bach with the pockets of his knickers turned inside out - his protest of the poor wages for artists and musicians.

My pockets hold my hands when I am tired and a little lonely for the feeling of corduroy or someone's hand to hold. ✦

Simple Gifts: Peek-a-Boo

Our lives are woven with hellos and goodbyes. Sometimes the hellos are insincere interruptions like a spam caller hawking insurance or junk mail inviting you to consider pre-purchasing cremation services. More often, the hellos are good things, the exciting mystery of a new conversation, a new day, a new adventure. Goodbyes? Well, no one needs to be reminded of those. Goodbyes have thunder. Even now, the sound of goodbyes pounds on the corridors of blood and nerves between our temples with names and faces and memories.

Life has an order we are taught. Birth and Death. Hello and Goodbye. But what if...we are not wrong about the content only the order? What if life is full of goodbyes and hellos? We grieve. We mourn. We rise and greet whatever and whoever the new day brings. Goodbyes are necessary and often awful. Hellos are equally vital. What if a hello was meant to come after every goodbye? What would peek-a-boo be without the opening of closed hands over a face that smiles its hello over and over again?

Goodbyes are gut-wrenching times of change and loss. We comfort our faces in our hands and hide for a while, for as long as it takes to find the courage to open our faces to say hello. I know the season in which we find ourselves is not as simple as a child's game of peek-a-boo. But what if, just for today, we changed the order of our lives from hello and goodbye to goodbye and hello? What would it harm just for today to move through the day from goodbye to hello? What if changing the order made a difference? What if playing peek-a-boo with the morning sun is simply good for a chuff of breath, the muscle memory of a laugh and a smile of the child we all once were.

Let's play!

Peek-a-boo! Hello there, little one. ✦

Questions to consider:

1. What stood out for you in this pocket essay?

2. What thoughts or memories surfaced from your own experience?

3. What simple gift similar or different in your own life did this essay evoke for you?

Reader's Notes

Reader's Notes

Reader's Notes

Reader's Notes

Reader's Notes

Reader's Notes

Acknowledgements

The more deeply I live, the more I plant my feet in the soil of gratitude. For decades, I have written an electronic devotional called ELOGOS which still enjoys a loyal following of some formers students and friends. I am grateful for having these patient and gracious readers in my life.

Garrett Sampson is one of those long-time ELOGOS subscribers. We have never met in person but, from his perch in Minnesota, Garrett has encouraged and supported my writing and art. I am grateful for his friendship, generosity and good humor.

Lisa Hoelscher is a student from my campus ministry days. Her journey since then included church work, seminary studies and forming a household with her husband Danny and their two daughters. She is now a pastor and I am proud to call her my colleague and friend. With this book, she became my trusted editor. No garbage bag full of fuchsia pens could outweigh my gratitude for the privilege of such a witty, gifted, class-act-of-a- person in my life. ✦

About the Author

Deb Grant is a human living under the laws of gravity in Houston, Texas. Grant is the author of 8 previous books, Pedestrian Theology, ELOGOS Daily Devotions for Down to Earth Disciples 1, 2, & 3, Passage: Lenten Devotions, Storm, Nuevo Vino and contributing author to Beacon Hunters.

A native of New England, Grant earned her undergraduate degree from Barrington College (now Gordon College). She earned a Master of Divinity from Trinity Lutheran Seminary, Columbus, Ohio. Grant was ordained in 1981, serving as a pastor in the Evangelical Lutheran Church in America in Goodlettsville, Tennessee; Clemson, South Carolina; College Station, Texas and Dickinson, Texas. After 37 years in parish and campus ministry, Grant retired. She continues to write, create art pieces, care for her friends and use her art and words whenever possible for the greater good. Most of the time she is the humble servant to her dog and bird.

Deb Grant's Contact Information:

Email: revdeb@jazzwater.com

Websites: jazzwater.com

debgrant.substack.com

Etsy Shop: www.etsy.com/shop/Jazzwater

Facebook: elogosbydebgrant

Instagram: jazzwater

To purchase Deb Grant's books:

- Jazzwater.com
- Order from local independent bookstores
- Amazon.com

Other publications by Deb Grant:

The Jesse Tree*(Creative Communication for the Parish)*

Pedestrian Theology*(Langmarc Publishing)*

ELOGOS Daily Devotions for Down to Earth Disciples. Volumes 1, 2, & 3.

Passage: Lenten Devotions

Storm

Nuevo Vino

Beacon Hunters (Grant, Hoelscher, Meier)

Available at Jazzwater.com or Amazon.com

www.ingramcontent.com/pod-product-compliance
Lightning Source LLC
Chambersburg PA
CBHW062146020426
42334CB00020B/2539